I'm just a girl

Berri Nguyen

BookLeaf
Publishing

India | USA | UK

Presentation by *BookLeaf Publishing*

Web: www.bookleafpub.com

E-mail: info@bookleafpub.com

ISBN: 9789363310964

First edition 2024

To mom and dad,

*Thanks for trusting me, I know can be a whole
lot to handle!*

PREFACE

I intended this book for every girl out there who feels like they experiencing life alone. Trust me, there are many people out here living with the same experience with you whether if it's about feeling excluded from your friend group or going through a very hard heartbreak. You are not alone.

I'm just a girl

I'm a girl
I'm dramatic and crazy
And I go extremely mad when people call me
lazy
I'm a girl
Being called pretty was all that I wanted
Yet once I hear it I never believe it
I'm a girl
I will take things personally
I get my anger and sadness out through either
song or my journal
I'm a girl
I yearn to be understood deeply
Someone who won't judge and care for my heart
like their kidney
I'm a girl
My feelings exist to be felt, and written out
Feels and write things I couldn't say out loud
I'm a girl
My biggest opponent is time
I want to be and do so many things while don't
have a dime
I'm a girl
My worst fear is to be forgotten
Like a tangerine that rotten

I'm a girl
I have a connection with a pomegranate
Where every little part of me is all together like
a soulmate
I'm a girl
I want to be seen as more than just a girl
I want to be compared to
I want to be looked up to
I want to be respected.

Hopeless

Born to be a poem
Forced to be a poet
Wanted to be written through adoration
Ended up writing out of the fear of being
forgotten

Born to be a hopeless romantic
Forced to master detachment
Because I fall for the wrong people for the
wrong reasons
I fall for books and movie expectations
I fall for all the simple acts that got romanticized
from my delusion
So I forced myself to detach as a solution.
Even if that means I have to put up with more
protection
Even if that means I have to break connections
And even If I can't let go of the attachment
I will force myself to hold on to the obsession
Until my life considered that connection as an
abomination.

Forced to be a writer
Born to be a muse

I write the world as I see it through my
red-tinted lens
Full of surprises and full of pretends
And I wish someone would look at me
Through the eyes as blue as the sea
As desperate as that sounds
I feel the world through a heart with open
wounds
So my eyes had to protect my heart
Living in the cloud so I don't get hurt.

The kid in me

5

I don't think the kid in me ever left
She's in there haunting a part of me
Like the gum under the desk
I can feel her in my chest
Whenever anyone slightly raises their voice
I can see her sitting in the corner
Cover her ear to stop the noise
my tears running down faster
As I start seeing a child hiding to seek help
a child who looked just like me when I was
younger
Now become a girl who trying to be held
There's a bridge connecting them
A hug from momma does it pretty well

I was once a mature kid
Always act right and know my limits
Now I'm just a childish girl
With no protection from expectations from the
world.

Memories

Memories are like sand at the beach.
Endlessly uncountable
And barely controllable
Once in a full moon when you look back
Whether in your clothes or your bag
You will find them hiding in the corner
And it will bring back memories that were just a blur
Memories that were forgotten
Just like fruit that is rotten.

Eternal Sunshine

Oh to love and to be loved
A process of fulfilling that will never be enough
To love is to give
You give every part of you away
The pain and joy of your day
The pride and shame of your story
To have someone to stay through the peace and
the glory
To love is to fear
Like gambling in a casino
You sacrifice so much just to be known
And all that is left is the fear of losing
Losing something that seems like everything

But frankly,
In this game of love, we are all losing
Losing the game that I wasn't sure that I wanted
to be winning
Because what does it mean to win
Am I winning because I love more and i lost
more
Or am I winning because I didn't love enough so
I rarely lost anything?
The game that I wasn't sure I was even playing
I just give all I had and then regret

And now you are running in my head
Repeating all the words that you've said
All the memories that won't stop to spread
Still, you're a part that my heart doesn't want to
forget

Even when my body doesn't react to your scent
My ears don't acknowledge your voice
My eyes don't notice your appearance
My lips don't crave your kisses
And my brain no longer has any information
about you
My heart still lingers at first glance
You have a look that makes me want to choose
romance.

Frankly again,
Love is never at first glance
Because I brought you so much pain
Whether it its got you sick from running in the
rain
Or accidentally step on your shoes when we
danced
Whether I ignore you when you are complaining
Or when I left because we were screaming
I removed all traces of those memories
Thinking it would help me move on quickly
But my heart still crave your existence
It desired me to run back to where "us" existed

Like we have a string between us
Slow us down in a world full of rushes
Once again, I'm falling in love
I fall for every part you hate about yourself
And I love you with every part I love about
myself
So moral of the story,
Love is worth the risk
To love and lose
To give and forgive
To cry and die
To commit to a soul that isn't yours
To acknowledge the consequences of love
And then choose it anyway
Because to be loved and lost
Is better than never being loved at all
Love is risky and scary
But so is everything else
So, Enjoy it!

Made with love

I was made with love
And made to love

I was taught to love
To love with my whole heart
Be the light shining for people in the dark
To love everything and anything
To give love no matter what people are offering

I was taught with love.
From people who get homesick from their lover
From people who believe in forever after
With affections and fairy tales
With love above all the scales

I was made with love
The love that I never get
Yet I still love with the love I always wanted
And giving love is still never my regrets
Because I know there's always someone who
needs it

I was made to love unconditionally.
With the sunset or 7 am coffee
With my heart broken or fully healed

I love like a little kid running down the hill
Freely with no fear in her head
Because love will burn like a cigarette
So might as well just do it and then regret it.
-With love, As always.

I'm my father's daughter

Unfortunately, I am my father's daughter
So I will not express my feelings
I will most likely just stare at the ceiling
Escape the reality with even more thinking

I am my father's daughter.
So I will let my anger build up until it explodes
Screaming as my emotions overflow
This time I don't do it like my father does though
I scream out of fear
The fear of being screamed at.

I am my father's daughter.
So I will love my mom with all my heart
Love her through all the thick and thin
The easy and the hard
From time to time
Because as a daughter I have so much love
But as a human, I have so much anger.
I think it's normal though
Because I'm a teenager
A kid living with so little experiences
Yet she believes she deserves better.

Maybe in another universe

Maybe in another life
We could do everything we ever planned
We could be jamming out
While the world listens to the rain
Maybe I would like just do taxes and laundry
with you
Maybe we could have been each other's home
Knowing there's someone always waiting for
you to run back to
But yet it's a maybe
Because maybe I'm on your mind just as much
as you've been on mine
Think about us and ask yourself
"Imagine if we tried?"
It's a maybe
Because maybe my efforts to hold on to this
delusion are worth it
Even though it feels like hugging a cactus
I would still hold on tighter than ever
Even if I bleed out
But it's forever a maybe
Because I'm in love with the impossibility of us
While you were looking at me with lust
It's a maybe
Because maybe in another universe

Our hearts will ache at the same time
And I don't have to scroll on tik tok
Hoping to find a video that says
"This is your sign"
Maybe in another universe
Our voices would echo in each other minds
Except this time it doesn't feel like a headache
anymore.
Maybe in another universe
Our glimpse would meet in a crowded room
My heart bloomed as you smile
And once again we would feel like the only two
alive
Maybe in another universe
We are two stars shining in the sky
Instead of being a moon a star,
We both shine so brightly right across each
other
And yet we only cross once in a while
And then continue to part ways
Maybe in another universe
Even though I really wanted it to be this one.

To be loved

To be loved is to be known
Oh to have somebody know your favorite
cologne
Or just how you want to be texted on the phone
Somebody who remembers your favorite candy
Or just how you think cherry flavor stuff is nasty
Somebody who remembers your shoe size
Or remember how badly you can handle spice
Somebody who knows your favorite flowers
So they could get you a bouquet with every
color
Somebody who knows how you want to be held
So they could comfort you with the love you
deserve
Somebody who knows your trauma and pain
Just so they could love you more all over again
Somebody who has seen all your scars
So they could cover them with kisses and stars
Somebody who listens to your inner child
So they could love you gently
So they could prove to you your love is worthy
And so they could prove loving you is easy
Because you were never hard to love.

Would you ?

Would you love me in every lifetime
When you're rich or barely have a dime
Whether you've stayed the same or changed into
a new person
Whether we meet in a different location

Would you love me in every lifetime
When life isn't worth living
So our soul brings us together
United in another universe?

Would you love me in every lifetime
When you are a human and I'm just a bird
Would you take me in when I fell and got hurt
Or would you ignore me on the sidewalk

Would you love me in every lifetime
When we were stranded in the city
Don't know where to go or what to do to be
happy
Will you unconsciously go back to where we
were
Where everything feels right

Would you love me in every lifetime

Would you let me go to find my dream
Yet admiring me for my success
With the same unconditional love

Would you love me in a lifetime
When I'm salt and you're water
Would you want me to blur into you
Or stay away so you don't taste bitter

Would you love me in every lifetime
When the heartbeat no longer has impulse
When metal and wire are up to the rule
Would you reject your system
Just to fall for me and ignore all problems?

Would you love me in every lifetime?
Would your hand stuck to the notebook
Blindly drawing my shadow when you were
dreaming
Until you find a tint of my skin
Until you see a glimpse of my eyes
And fall in love before we even say hi

Would you find me in every lifetime?

Growing up

Growing up never feels harder
When you change every single chapter
Life after 10 flows so much faster
Make me questioning
if it's really for the better?

Is it for the better?
Because I lost people who I wished were my
soulmate
Lost them when I was not mature enough to
appreciate
Lost them when I was looking for more
Even though all I needed was waiting at the door

Is it really for the better?
If I didn't know how little I would look at me
Would she be scared of my look
or would she think I'm pretty?
Because the mirror reflects someone I don't
know
Yet changes feel more comforting
Even though the only thing that stayed the same
was my shadow

Is it really for the better

When I know I'm not a horrible person
I'm just 15, a hot mess with so much passion
Stuck in a cycle of wanting to get better
Creatures of habitual torture
Stuck between too young and too old
To do anything and everything.

Please

I wanted to be loved by you so bad
Because you all that I had
So now I'm on my knees begging
Don't forget my drinks order, please
I still remember yours
Don't forget my family, please
I still remember yours
Don't forget my house address, please
I still remember your
Don't forget my favorite candy, please
I still remember
Don't forget me plea
I won't ever forget you
I wish we never stopped talking
But we did.

We stopped talking

We stopped talking
I walked by our coffee shop today
The owner still asked if you are doing okay
We stopped talking
I listened to our band's new releases
Except this time you're no longer next to me
We stopped talking
I saw a hoodie in your favorite color
I had to resist myself from thinking how good it
would look on you
We stopped talking
Today I accidentally ordered your favorite drinks
A thought of you made my heart sink
Just a tiny bit
We stopped talking
Snapchat reminded me of videos we took a year
ago
Made me wonder why you let me go
We stopped talking
My heart froze as I hear a voice
That sounds just like you
We stopped talking
A random wrap of candy was found in my bag
You left your pieces behind to haunt me every
day

We stopped talking
And God, I miss talking to you.

Kids ≠ Adults

As kids
We find comfort and joy in nothing.
And as adults,
We find nothing in everything.

As a kid, I wanted to be a hero
To save the world
As I get older, I want to be saved from the
world
Because I realized I won't ever be anyone's hero
Not even myself.

In a complex world
Where the dissatisfaction with myself constantly
lingers,
I found joy in the tiniest and simplest things in
life
Hoping the fear of growing up will leave
Once I become a kid again

Things I grew out of

Things I grew out of
The bracelet I made in seventh grade
The swimsuit I wore in 2018 to the lake
The Converse I walked through every corner in
The Mario Kart game that I never win
The Oreo milkshake I always ordered
The jacket my mom made me wear once it got
colder
All the songs I thought were my anthem
Hugging my mom until my arms go numb
That shirt I wore until it turned gray
Having a big party for my birthday
The friendship I thought was forever
The people in my last life chapter

I guess life will never be how we want it to be
Things can feel like forever yet they'll leave
when you aren't ready
So sometimes I order that milkshake again
Wear that Converse despite the pain
Just to relive the feelings of yesterday
To reconnect with everything I lost along the
way
To see my best friend who I thought would
always stay
But now I can't even reach out to say "Hey".

Thank you

Thanks for loving me when I didn't love myself
When life was horrible
And I struggle to stay alive
Wondering if I'm loveable
Thanks for caring for me when I did not know
how to care for myself
For putting a blanket on me when I'm sleeping
For wiping my tears when they're running
Thanks for being kind to me when I wasn't kind
to myself
For telling me words that calm my heart
For giving me affection whenever I'm hurt
Thanks for listening to the little girl in me
Shehe has so much anger and sorrow
Yet you loved her so gently
Andso passionately like there was no tomorrow.

Who are you?

You are the second mom of the family
You took care of everyone
Part-time sister
Full-time family take care
You were always easy to raise
We just won't talk about your struggles back in
the days
You were never a bother
Because you shut your mouth
 and try to be a perfect daughter
You were raised to become independent
So much that you refuse to believe anyone's
good intention
Or simply anyone who willing to give you
attention
You were always craving attention
So much that you secretly wished to become
sick
So your parents would care and ask you
questions
You were always jealous of a 4 years old kid
The kid that always has the love that you crave
So you had no choice but to look at it with
hatred
You were always struggling with love

You can't ever think you are enough
Taking care of people and you felt like a
competition
Where you both lose and win against your
person
Because the trophy has always been you
You were never anything close to what you
wished you were
You are an older sister.

7 years

Every 7 years
Your skin will recycle
And all your evidence in life will disappear

A part of me lit up knowing this
Because it means all the mistakes I made
All the pain that I did
To my body and myself with hate
Will be gone and disappear
Be gone with my skin soaked in tears

A part of me was saddened
Knowing all the scars I have will mean nothing
Including that scar you gave me that I didn't
want to heal
I wanted to have a part of you on me to look at
every morning
It makes the illusion in my head feel real
The illusion that you were once mine
Even when we already cut ties

Moon and Sun

The moon is pretty, isn't it?
She asked him
Her heart lights up thinking about him
Yet her mouth can't form a formal sentence to
express her love
Because in her own eyes, she was never good
enough
He's a sun in her eyes
So far away up in the sky
Shine brightly and so unreachable
Makes the chances between them impossible
Especially under the sun so bright
She's comfortably burning under his light
All she wanted was to be closer to him.

The sunset is pretty, isn't it?
He replied,
A thought of her saddened his heart
Her voice replayed like a song in his head
She's the fall leaves on the pavement
So fragile and elegant
And he's hurting her if he comes close
So last thing he did for the girl he loves the most
He lets her go.

To me

Dear myself
Growing up means realizing.
Imperfect is the perfect that we don't see
The scar on my knee from dancing
The smile line from surrounded by good people
The wrinkles from aging as the world continues
to keep spinning
Imperfections are just proof of experiences

The mistakes you made along the way
The friend that you outgrew yesterday
The unerasable scars on your arms
The words that you said when you weren't calm
Painfully remarkable yet bittersweet
Mistakes Are just evidence of humanity

Life after all is never about chasing perfection
It's about living without the desire to be known
It's about making peace with yourself until your
head feels like home
It's about loving your image like how you would
love your soulmate
It's about learning to understand yourself
without wishing to be understood
It's about being imperfect.